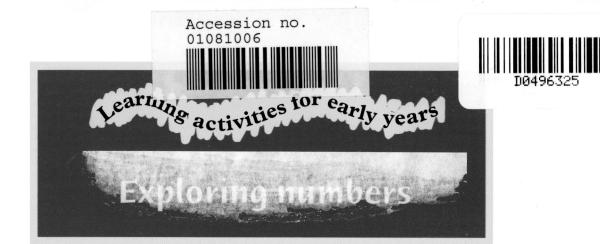

Learning activities for early years

Exploring numbers

# Janine Blinko

Illustrations by Alison Dexter
Photographs by Zul Mukhida

# Contents

A & C Black • London

# Introduction

The National Numeracy Strategy *Framework for teaching mathematics* (DfEE, 1999) and *Early Learning Goals* (QCA, 1999) emphasise what has long been recognised: that practical activity, discussion and focused teaching are the triple key to understanding mathematics. Providing the right equipment is not enough on its own. Children learn mathematics best if it is presented in an enjoyable way and discussed with skilled and informed questioning from the teacher.

*Exploring numbers* offers a number curriculum specifically for nursery and reception aged children. It makes particular reference to the early learning goals and the National Numeracy Strategy learning objectives for Reception. The activities are designed to allow children to do mathematics for themselves, and to think about, discuss and develop their own ideas so that when they go on to Year 1, they will know how to tackle the subject with confidence and have a sound foundation on which to build.

Children of this age are a particular joy to teach because of their excitement and enthusiasm for learning. The teacher should make the most of this by providing an exciting and varied environment in which children can explore number through a range of contexts.

At first, the teacher's role is to interject with questions that move children's thinking forward in the course of their play. If a child makes two model people in Plasticine, the teacher might ask, 'If I make one more, how many will there be?' or 'You have made two people, so how many legs are there all together?' When children are at the stage where they can respond appropriately to such questions, it is time to structure their learning more tightly with some clear learning goals.

The activities in this book aim to build on the children's early 'free' experiences and focus their thinking more closely on the mathematics in which they are involved.

It is important to emphasise that skilled questioning is crucial to activities that are both structured and unstructured. With careful discussion, a dialogue will develop where teacher and children ask and respond to questions with growing understanding.

## How to use this book

*Exploring numbers* is organised in units, each of which includes an introduction that explains the areas of mathematics covered by the activities in the unit and their extensions.

## Differentiation

It is not expected that all children will experience all the activities in a unit. Within any activity, some children might be meeting a mathematical idea for the first time; others may be consolidating their understanding by applying it in a new context.

All the activities include extension ideas for those children who have demonstrated sound understanding in the main task. There are also suggestions for varying the activities for those children who need to consolidate their ideas by doing something again in a slightly different context (for example, by changing the numbers). Most of the activities have the potential for extension or simplification by changing the range of numbers offered to the children, or by providing fewer or more clues.

## Assessing the children's learning

The main method of assessment is observing how children cope with the activities. The introduction to each unit highlights potential problem areas, while the assessment section

offers ideas for questions to ask the children and, occasionally, a specific assessment task. Every unit also includes responses from children as they have carried out the activities in the classroom. These observations may also be helpful for assessment purposes.

## Other quick ideas

These are activities for a spare five minutes. Requiring little or no preparation, they are an important way of presenting new ideas as well as consolidating understanding, and can soon become a regular, fun feature of the day.

## Involving parents

Each unit ends with some simple activities specifically designed for children and parents to enjoy together. It may be useful to inform parents of the learning intentions that the activities address. In some cases, particularly where the children are collecting information (for example, how many doors there are in their home), the results could be collated and used in school (for example represented on a sorting diagram).

The table below shows the connections between activities in this book, early learning goals for mathematical development and key objectives in the *Framework for teaching mathematics* for Reception. Some activities link with more than one goal or key objective; the teacher/trainer's questions and subsequent discussion with the children will provide the focus.

| Early Learning Goals and Key Objectives | Unit: Activities | |
|---|---|---|
| Say and use number names in order in familiar contexts; | **Counting:** Who's wearing the hat?; Stand up, sit down<br>**Order:** Lost steps; Names | **Odds and evens:** Whisper counts<br>**Recognising errors:** Missing; Pegs |
| count reliably up to 10 everyday objects; | **Counting:** Cup counting; Secret jumping<br>**Three:** all the activities | **Tens:** all the activities<br>**Money:** Shopping; Jumping pennies |
| recognise numerals 1 to 9; | **Recognising and writing symbols:** all the activities | **Recognising errors:** Pegs |
| use language such as 'more' or 'less', 'greater' or 'smaller', to compare two numbers; | **More or fewer?:** In a spin; Egg boxes; Hiding<br>**Order:** all the activities | **Estimating:** Sticks<br>**Odds and evens:** Cubes game |
| in practical activities and discussion, begin to use vocabulary involved in adding and subtracting; | **More or fewer?:** all the activities<br>**Estimating:** Potatoes<br>**Addition:** Fingers | **Subtraction:** Before; Act it out<br>**Finding the difference:** all the activities |
| find one more or one less than a number from 1 to 10; | **More or fewer?:** In a spin<br>**Order:** Hanging socks | **Odds and evens:** Cubes game |
| begin to relate addition to combining two groups of objects; | **Addition:** all the activities | |
| begin to relate subtraction to 'taking away'; | **Subtraction:** all the activities | |
| talk about, recognise and re-create simple patterns; | **Pattern:** all the activities<br>**Recognising errors:** Animal patterns | |
| use developing mathematical ideas and methods to solve practical problems. | **Counting:** Secret jumping<br>**More or fewer?:** Hiding<br>**Order:** Lost steps<br>**Three:** Making triangles<br>**Estimating:** all the activities | **Recognising and writing symbols:** Feely bag; Peep-bo; Who am I?<br>**Sorting:** all the activities<br>**Odds and evens:** Cubes game; Socks<br>**Money:** Special coins; A handful of coins |

# Counting

## Intended learning

To recite the number names in order to five (or ten); to recite the number names in order counting on and back from a given number; to count accurately a set of objects that can be seen, and a set that cannot be seen (for example, sounds); to begin to read numerals.

## Introduction

To be able to count, children need to understand both the cardinal and the ordinal aspects of counting. That is, they need to be able to learn the number names and say them in order, and also to know that the final number in the count represents the whole set of objects counted. If children experience difficulty in counting, it may be with one or both of these aspects.

With experience, children also develop the ability to recognise small quantities without counting, initially with two or three objects, but later with as many as seven or eight, depending on how the group of items is arranged. For example, children might come to recognise the arrangement of symbols on playing cards.

All the activities in this section are designed to develop children's ability to count initially to five, and then to ten. They can all be extended to counting beyond ten.

## Key vocabulary

**numbers, start, finish, different, next, last, repeat, count on, count back**

## Who's wearing the hat?

### Group size:
four to five children.

### You will need:
a hat from the dressing-up box or one made in advance from newspaper.

### The activity

As a warm-up, sit everyone in a circle and practise counting to five together.

Give one child the hat to wear, and ask him or her to start the counting by saying 'one'. The child to the left should say 'two', then the next child 'three', and so on until everyone in the group has said a number. Celebrate with a clap or a cheer! Next, choose a different child to wear the hat and begin the counting so that everyone's number changes.

Sometimes children will need a few practices or prompts before the count gets all the way back round to the person wearing the hat.

### Extension and differentiation

● Make the game simpler by playing with just three children.

● The child wearing the hat starts with a number other than one, and the children count on round the group from that number.

● The hat-wearer starts with the number of children in the group (for example, four if there are four children in the group), then the children count back down to one.

● Make one number 'special'. Whoever says that number may shout it out rather than just saying it.

● As each child says their number, let them put one counter in the middle of the group. Help them to understand that at the end of the count there should be as many counters as there are children.

● Give each child a set of number cards. Ask them not only to say the appropriate number as they count round the group, but also to find the appropriate number card.

Dropping pennies so that others can count as they fall

## Cup counting

### Group size:
up to ten children.

### You will need:
a cup; some pennies.

### The activity
Rhythmically drop the coins one at a time into the cup so that the children are unable to see them go in. Encourage all the children to listen carefully and count the coins silently as they drop. Ask if they can tell you how many coins are in the cup.

Repeat the process, trying a variety of irregular rhythms.

### Extension and differentiation
● Support children by letting them watch as the coins are dropped in.

● Give each child or pair of children a set of 0 to 5 number cards. Ask the children to find the appropriate number cards to show how many coins were dropped each time.

● Let the children take turns at dropping the coins in the cup.

● Try dropping just a few coins into the cup and establishing together how many there are. Then drop a few more and ask the children how many there are now.

● Drop a few coins into the cup and establish together how many there are. Then take a few out, telling the children how many you have taken. Ask them how many there are now.

## Stand up, sit down

### Group size:
up to ten children.

### You will need:
no special equipment.

### The activity
Get the children to stand in a circle. As a warm-up, ask them to count round the group up to four (one, two, three, four; one, two, three, four).

Repeat the process, but explain that this time whoever says 'four' should sit down and not join in the counting again until the end of the game. Then ask them to go round the circle again counting up to four, missing out the children sitting down. Once more, whoever says 'four' should sit down. When only three children are left, the child who says 'one' will also say 'four'. Continue until only one child is left standing. This child could be invited to start the next count.

### Extension and differentiation
● Try counting to a different number.

● Ask if any of the children can guess who will be the last person standing. Is it likely to be the same person each time? To predict the outcomes, the group will need to be systematic about where the counting starts. Encourage the children to remember who started the counting off and who was the last one standing. On the second round, let the person next to the first child start the counting. (If the counting is correct, the person next to the 'finisher' in the first round should be the last one standing.)

## Secret jumping

### Group size:
four to eight children.

### You will need:
a set of 1 to 5 number cards (or 1 to 9, depending on the ability of the children).

### The activity
In this game the teacher should be the leader for the first few turns, then the children can take over.

Let one child secretly choose a number card with you. Ask the child to jump on the spot in front of the other children the number of times shown on the card. Challenge the rest of the group to work out from the number of jumps what the secret number was.

### Extension and differentiation
● Let the children take turns to do a certain number of jumps (or claps, or steps, or 'la la la's), and encourage the others to count along.

● Invite the child with the number card to jump more quickly, more slowly or irregularly. Ask the rest of the group whether the number is still the same.

● Give each child their own set of number cards and ask them to hold up the correct number card for the number of jumps.

## Assessment

● Can the children recite the names of the numbers in the correct order?

● Do they know that the last word they say in a count is the name for the whole amount in the group?

● Do they know that whatever order they count a group of objects in, they end up with the same number?

● Can they count when they can hear objects but not see them (for example, pennies dropped into a cup in a regular or irregular rhythm)?

## Evidence of the children's learning

The children very much enjoyed the *Cup counting* game and frequently requested to play it. Many of the children were able to count the coins when they were dropped into the cup with a slower regular rhythm – several mouthed the counting as they went along. Fewer children could keep track of the counting when the coins were dropped more quickly or in an irregular rhythm. However, as the game was repeated over several days, it became a great challenge to 'keep up' and they were very excited and pleased with themselves when they succeeded.

The children were also invited to play the game with a friend. This was very popular and certainly supported the irregular counting, as they found it difficult to drop the coins in any other way!

## Other quick ideas

● Take every opportunity to demonstrate counting (how many children are in the group, here today, need a drink, and so on).

● Find time to count fingers, chairs, pencils, paintbrushes, toys in the play house, etc.

● Let the children decide how many items, such as books or pencils, are needed for an activity.

● Regularly 'read' the room, asking the children to count pictures, notices, coat pegs, shelves, doors, windows, curtains, and so on.

● Sing number rhymes with the children, such as '1, 2, 3, 4, 5, Once I caught a fish alive'.

● Count how many times the word 'Jack' occurs in the rhyme 'Jack and Jill went up the hill'. Try this with other rhymes and other words.

## Involving parents

Ask parents to help their children count how many rooms (or doors, cupboards, people, etc.) there are at home. Children could also count the number of bites in a slice of toast, or count the stairs as they go up and down them. Parents could ask the children if they think it will be the same number on the way down as it was on the way up.

# More or fewer?

## Intended learning

To begin to understand 'more', 'less' and 'fewer' as part of the vocabulary of addition and subtraction; to begin to understand addition as counting on and subtraction as counting back; to count a collection of objects.

## Introduction

'More', 'less', 'fewer' and 'same' are part of the language of comparison. 'Fewer' is a numerical term and is used to describe a group of objects ('There are fewer girls than boys in the football team'), while 'less' is a quantitative term, used to describe amounts ('I have less orange juice than you'). In everyday language the word 'less' is used more frequently, whatever the context, so you will need to use the word 'fewer' alongside it to give the children an opportunity to develop a clearer understanding of its more specific meaning in mathematics.

These activities use the mathematical concepts of 'more' and 'fewer' to develop children's understanding of the quantity that numbers represent, and use comparisons to develop adding and subtracting skills.

## Key vocabulary

more, less, fewer, same

## In a spin

### Group size:
six to ten children.

### You will need:
some interlocking cubes (or similar equipment); a more/fewer spinner (see illustration).

### The activity

Introduce the activity by dividing the children into two groups and inviting someone from each group to take a handful of cubes and make a tower. Ask the two children to put their towers side by side, and let the groups decide who has more cubes in their tower and who has fewer (or if they have the same number).

Spin the paperclip on the spinner. If the paperclip ends up on the 'more' side of the spinner, the group that has more cubes in their tower wins the round. Similarly if the paperclip lands on 'fewer', the group with fewer cubes in their tower wins the round. If both have the same number of cubes in their towers, they both win!

Ask two more children to make new towers. Repeat the activity until all the children have had a turn at making towers.

## Extension and differentiation

● Keep a score of the winners of each round. The children could do this for themselves by collecting a counter or a penny each time their group wins.

● Let the children play the game in pairs.

● Change the rules so that in order to win a child must be able to say how many more or fewer they have than their opponent. For example, if the spinner shows more, the child must say, 'I have two more cubes than you, so I win!' (or similar).

## Egg boxes

### Group size:
six to eight children.

### You will need:
two or three egg boxes; small items for counting (such as beads or dried pasta).

### The activity
Arrange the egg boxes end-to-end. Divide the children into two groups. Invite one child from each group to take some beads and place them one at a time in the compartments of the boxes to make a line. Ask the children to make up a sentence to say whether they have more or fewer beads in their line than the other group.

*The children arranged the egg boxes end-to-end and filled the compartments in a line.*

## Extension and differentiation

● Invite the children to play the game in pairs.

● Ask the children to count the number of objects in each row and to use the numbers in their sentence, for example, 'I have five beads and Jo has seven, so she has more than me,' or 'I have five beads and Jo has seven, so I have two fewer than she has.'

# Caterpillars

## Group size:
four children.

## You will need:
a caterpillar drawing on card for each player; about 35 paper circles or large counters corresponding to the size of the circles on the caterpillars; several sets of game cards, as shown.

| 1 FEWER | 1 MORE |
|---------|--------|
| 2 FEWER | 2 MORE |
| 3 FEWER | 3 MORE |

## The activity

Give each player a caterpillar picture. Shuffle the game cards and place them face down. Ask the players to take turns to remove a game card from the top of the pile, then either collect the appropriate number of circles and place them on the segments of their caterpillar (for example, one more), or remove the appropriate number of circles from their caterpillar (for example, two fewer). Encourage the children to count on and back.

To begin with, the children might not have enough circles to remove, in which case you could make up a rule (for example, just remove what you have or miss a turn). The first player to cover all the circles of their caterpillar wins the game.

## Extension and differentiation

● Ask questions to encourage the children to talk about their caterpillars after each round ('Who has most circles?' 'How many circles do you have?' 'How many more do you need?' 'How many will you have if you add three more?').

● Make the caterpillars longer and make more cards with larger numbers on.

# Hiding

## Group size:
four to eight children.

## You will need:
a collection of small objects (such as cubes, counters, conkers or shells); something to use as a screen (such as a large book); two containers (such as cups).

## The activity

Count out the objects, giving the same number to yourself as to the group of children. Establish that you have the same number. Put each set of objects in a container and place a screen in front of them. Tell the children you are going to put two more items in their collection. Ask them which set has more now. Remove the screen and count the objects to check.

## Extension and differentiation

● Play the same game, but remove objects instead of adding them.

● Ask how many items they begin with. How many are there if some are added or removed?

## Assessment

● Can the children say whether they have more objects in their collection than you?

● Can they say whether anyone else has more than them?

## Evidence of the children's learning

The discussion during *Caterpillars* was particularly enlightening. For the first few games, all the questions were teacher-led, and the children were so engaged in their own caterpillars that they needed much encouragement to see how other players were getting on. During the fourth game, however, three out of the four children were making comparisons without being asked. Tim said, 'Look! I've got more than Beth! It's two more – can you see?'; Rhian said, 'If I get three more, then I'll have more than you, you and you'; and Sutan said, 'I need lots more to catch up with anyone!'

## Other quick ideas

● Ask all the children with white socks to stand together, and all the children with grey socks to stand together. Ask whether there are more or fewer children with grey socks. To test this, pair up the children wearing white socks with the children wearing grey socks. Ask them how many children are left over, and what colour socks they are wearing.

● Deliberately hand out too few pencils or pieces of paper, so that the children have to ask for more. This could be developed into a class joke! Ask, 'How many more do you need?'

● Talk about times when it is best to have fewer than anyone else (chicken pox spots, spiders in the bath, wasps in the kitchen, and so on).

● Let the children work in pairs. Call out, 'Show your fingers!', at which they should hold up a number of fingers. Ask them to say whether they are holding up more or fewer fingers than their partner. Develop this by calling out, 'Ready, steady... more!' or 'Ready, steady... fewer!', at which the children should hold up their fingers as before. Whichever child in each pair is holding up more or fewer (depending on what was said) wins.

## Involving parents

Ask parents to help their children find out 'more and fewer' facts about their home: for example, whether there are more windows than doors, whether there are more cars than teddies, whether there are more lights than light switches, and so on.

# Order

## Intended learning

To use the vocabulary of comparing and ordering numbers of objects; to use the vocabulary of ordinal numbers (first, second, third, and so on); to order a sequence of numbers of objects; to be able to say a number which lies between two others; to order selected numbers of objects.

## Introduction

Ordering is an extension of comparison. With two sets of objects to compare, the group with the smaller number has 'fewer', and the other group has 'more'. With more than two sets, the group with the smallest number of objects has 'fewest', and the group with the highest number of objects has 'most'. Once children can identify which of two groups has more ('Are there more biscuits on this plate or on the other?'), they will start to need experience of ordering more than two groups ('Can you put the plates in order of the number of biscuits?'). For some children, it is sufficient to begin by ordering just three groups of objects. As well as ordering with consecutive numbers, children need to be able to order groups that are not consecutive (for example, 3, 5, 8, 9). Each of the activities in this unit can be adjusted to give the children more or fewer numbers to order.

## Key vocabulary

**number names, before, after, next, last, missing, between, order, first, second, third, fourth, fifth, fewest, most**

## Lost steps

### Group size:
four or five children.

### You will need:
interlocking cubes.

### The activity
Arrange towers of one, two, three, four and five interlocking cubes to look like steps. Display them in front of the whole group.

Introduce the activity by talking about the steps ('What do you notice about the steps of cubes?' 'Can anyone find the step that has three cubes? Four? Two?' 'Which step has the most cubes?' 'Which has the fewest?'). Point to a step and ask: 'How many cubes are in the step after this one?' 'How many cubes are in the step before this one?'

Ask the children to close their eyes while you remove one of the steps. Ask the children how many cubes were in the step that has been taken away. If someone answers correctly, ask how they knew ('How did you work it out?' 'Did it help that the cubes were in a staircase?' 'How did it help?').

### Extension and differentiation
● Play the game with only three steps (one, two and three cubes).

● Invite the children to work in pairs and make their own staircase up to five cubes high. They can then play the same game amongst themselves.

● Add one extra cube to a step while the children close their eyes. Ask them which step has the extra cube.

# Names

## Group size:
about six children.

## You will need:
strips of 5cm squared paper cut to lengths of about 10 squares; pencils; scissors.

## The activity
Ask the children each to write their own name along a strip of paper with each letter in a separate square. Help them as necessary. Ask them to cut off any empty squares at the end of the strip.

Explain to the children that you want them to find out how many letters are in their name by counting the squares on their strip.

The children enjoyed comparing the lengths of their names.

Ask the children questions: 'Has anyone else got the same number of letters as you?' 'Have you got more or fewer letters than the person next to you?' 'Who has more letters than Rebecca?' 'Does anyone have fewer letters in their name than Amy?'

Note: when comparing lengths of their name strips, the children may need to be encouraged to hold them together at the first or last letter.

## Extension and differentiation

● Sort the names with the same number of letters into groups.

● Ask the children to place all the names in order of how many letters they have. If necessary, guide them to start with the longest name (or the shortest) and so on. Ask similar questions to those asked in the main activity.

# Hanging socks

## Group size:
five or six children.

## You will need:
some clean socks; a box of cubes; a wire coathanger; clothes pegs.

## The activity
Explain to the children that you are going to hide some cubes in a sock. Without the children seeing, put two, three or four cubes into the sock. Invite the children to take turns to feel the sock to try to decide how many cubes are in it. When some agreement has been reached, tip out the cubes to check.

Play the game several times, then place different numbers of cubes in, say, five socks. Let the children feel the socks and guess how many cubes are in each one. As a group, peg the socks in order along a wire coathanger.

## Extension and differentiation
● Prepare just three socks with one, two and three cubes. Peg them on a coathanger in any order. Invite children to put the socks in order.

● Let the children prepare their own socks with up to ten cubes. When they have worked out how many cubes are in each other's socks, let them peg them in order along the wire coathanger. If two or more socks hold the same number of cubes, let the children decide what to do with them. They may choose to use only one of them, use both of them, change one, etc.

● Ask the children to write the number of cubes in each sock on a sticky note and attach it to the sock as a label.

## Assessment

● Can children put groups of objects in order of quantity (remembering that 'in order' can mean smallest to largest or vice versa)?

● Can they order consecutive groups of one, two, three and four objects?

● Can they order consecutive groups of four, five, six and seven objects?

● Can they order non-consecutive groups of objects, for example, seven, three, five and two?

## Evidence of the children's learning

In *Lost steps* in particular it was interesting to watch the children learn from each other. There were two main strategies that the children employed to find out which step was missing. Some children used the fact that each step was 'one more' than the previous one, so they would comment when there was a step of two more than the last. This strategy still worked when it was the first step that was 'lost'. The second strategy was to count the cubes in each step. 'One; one, two; one, two, three, four – that's not right!' said Tom. Tom went on to make a three-cube step and checked by counting again: 'One; one, two; one, two, three; one, two, three, four.' Kris, who was next, tried to copy this strategy but failed because he could not remember what the previous step had been! The next child, Luke, used the same technique successfully.

## Other quick ideas

● Ask three children to hold up any number of fingers. Put the children in order according to how many fingers they are showing.

● Invite three children in the group each to take a handful of cubes or counters. Discuss with the group who has the most and who has the fewest. Let them decide how many each child has, and who has more than whom.

● Put the piles of cubes or counters in order from the smallest number to the largest or the largest to the smallest.

● Give the children a number card each and ask them to put themselves in order according to their number. You may need to ask encouraging questions ('Who should be first?' 'Who should be next to you?').

● Give the children number cards and let one child put all the others in order.

## Involving parents

Suggest that at dinner-time, parents let their children order the plates according to how many potatoes are on them. Encourage other ordering activities. For example, sort a bag of coloured sweets by colour. Arrange the sets of colours in order of the number of sweets in each group. Eat some, then rearrange the groups as necessary. Children could also make towers with building bricks so that each tower has one more brick than the previous one.

# Three

## Intended learning

To count a collection of objects with accuracy; to count in a range of contexts; to learn number names; to understand the conservation of number.

## Introduction

One of the hurdles children need to overcome is understanding that however a group of objects is arranged, the number of objects remains unchanged. This is known as the conservation of number. Three is used as the example here, but the same is true of all numbers. These activities also introduce the ordinal aspect of number (three comes before four and after two), and how the symbol 3 is used to represent a range of ideas ('I am three'; 'It is three o'clock'; 'I went on a number 3 bus') and a range of sizes (three oranges; three boxes of oranges; three lorry-loads of boxes of oranges, and so on). The following *Three* activities can all be adapted for any other number up to nine.

## Key vocabulary

number names, three, triangle, too many, too few, more, fewer

## Boxes

### Group size:
four to eight children.

### You will need:
an assortment of different-sized boxes.

### The activity

Ask the children to work in pairs and choose three boxes. Ask them to arrange their boxes to make the longest line they can. Compare the lengths of the lines each pair has made.

Develop this by asking the children to use their three boxes to make the shortest line they can; the tallest tower they can; the wiggliest line they can; a line as near as possible to the length of their foot, arm, hand, leg, and so on.

After the children have completed each task, discuss and compare the lines they have made ('Could anyone have made their line longer, shorter, closer to the right length?').

### Extension and differentiation

● Reinforce the idea that the children have used only three boxes, no matter how long their lines are.

● Ask each pair of children to repeat the activity using three different boxes.

● Let them work alone instead of in pairs.

● Let the children experiment with different numbers of boxes.

Making triangles from strips of paper

# Making triangles

## Group size:
four to eight children.

## You will need:
strips of paper or straws of different lengths; display paper; glue.

## The activity
Introduce the activity by discussing what a triangle is. Ask the children each to choose three strips of paper and use them to make a triangle. Discuss their triangles with them: 'Which were pointy?' 'Which was the biggest?' 'Which was the smallest?' 'Did anyone have three strips that couldn't be used to make a complete triangle (one very long strip with two short strips)?' Invite them to try again with three different strips of paper.

Display the triangles by sticking them on to a large sheet of coloured paper.

## Extension and differentiation
● Support any children having difficulty with the activity by only providing strips of paper of a size suitable for making a triangle (i.e. by removing all the very long and very short strips).

● Let the children work in small groups of three or four. Ask them to take turns to roll a dice and collect that number of paper strips. After three rounds ask the children to use their strips to make as many triangles as they can. The child with the most triangles wins the game.

## Step game

### Group size:
six to ten children.

### You will need:
a set of game cards showing different kinds of walking; chalk or two skipping ropes.

fairy steps | giant steps | ordinary steps
crouched steps | twirly steps | penguin steps

### The activity
Practise doing each of the steps with the children.

Use the chalk or the ropes to mark a start line and a finish line on the floor, 3–4 metres apart. Then mix up the cards and place them face down where the children can see them.

Ask the children to stand on the start line. Turn over the top card and show it to the first child. Ask the child to make three of the steps shown on the card towards the finish line. Put the card to the bottom of the pile, then show the next card to the second child, and so on until all the children have had a turn. When all the cards have been used, shuffle them and start the pile again. The first child to cross the finish line wins the game.

Note: you may need to 'fix it' if some children constantly have to move in small steps.

### Extension and differentiation
● Reduce the number of different types of steps if desired.

● Let the children invent other sorts of steps and make new cards to include in the set. These could be turning steps, waddling, hopping, skipping, etc.

● Let the children turn over a card to find out what type of steps they should do, then roll a dice to find out how many.

## Threes on paper

### Group size:
four to eight children.

### You will need:
lots of different-sized pieces of paper, from stamp-sized to A3.

### The activity
Ask each child to choose one piece of paper. Explain to the children that you would like them to find three items from around the room (not necessarily three of the same thing) that

will fit on their piece of paper without any overlapping, or bits hanging over the edges. Discuss the items the children choose ('Did anyone use three things the same?' 'Did anyone use one big thing and two small ones? Two big and one small?' 'Did anyone use anything circular?' 'What were the easiest shapes to use?' 'Could anyone swap their things to fit on someone else's piece of paper?').

Let the children repeat the activity with another piece of paper.

## Extension and differentiation

● Ask the children to use a different-sized piece of paper. Can they still use the same three things?

● Ask the children to find three things to cover as much of the paper as possible without objects overlapping or hanging over the edge.

## Assessment

● Can the children count objects that are close together?

● Can they count the same objects if they are spaced far apart?

● Can they tell you how many there are without counting a second time? (This indicates that they can appreciate the conservation of number in this instance.)

● Can they make collections of threes of different-sized objects, such as three grains of rice, three chairs, even three children? (This will indicate that the children appreciate that 'threeness' is not related to size.)

## Evidence of the children's learning

The children were very particular about the number of steps others made in the *Step game*, watching the moves very carefully. They also became very interested in the completeness of the steps, making comments such as, 'That's not three – that's three and a little bit more,' and 'Do a bit more – that's not quite three full ones.' They were also fascinated by *Threes on paper*, saying things like, 'I didn't know three could be so big!'

## Other quick ideas

● Ask the children to get themselves into groups of three, then to change to different groups of three, and so on.

● Ask the children to show you three fingers, then a different three fingers, and so on.

● Let the children find three things each, then compare what they have found.

● Invite children to look around the room and find collections of three, such as three fish in the tank, three flowers on a plant, three pencils on the floor, and so on.

## Involving parents

Ask parents to let their children find the correct cutlery to lay the table for three people, three bears or three Billy-Goats-Gruff; that is, three knives, three forks and three spoons. Children could also make collections of three big, three small and three medium-sized things.

# Estimating

## Intended learning

To estimate a number and check by counting; to count reliably a collection of objects; to begin to recite number names beyond ten.

## Introduction

As well as being able to count (and calculate) accurately, children need to develop a sense of whether or not answers are reasonable. One indication of how the children's number sense is expanding is the development of their ability to estimate quantities. Many estimating activities may be built into other number activities by the use of questions: 'How many do you think there are?' 'How many steps do you think we shall need?' 'How many buttons do you think there are?' 'Have you got enough?' However, this section offers more structured activities aimed at developing children's ability and willingness to estimate.

## Key vocabulary

guess, close, estimate,
number names

## Sticks

### Group size:
four to eight children.

### You will need:
interlocking cubes.

### The activity

Make a 'stick' of interlocking cubes, long enough for three or four of the cubes to be visible to one side of your clenched hand when you hold it. (Holding the stick in a clenched hand prevents the children from seeing all the cubes.)

Hold the stick up and ask the children how many cubes they think are in it, including the ones that are hidden in your hand. Ask questions to help them along ('How big are the cubes?' 'Do you think I could hide more than one cube in my hand?' 'Could I hide ten?' 'How many can you see?' 'Do you think there are more than that hiding?'). Count the cubes together. How close were the children's guesses?

### Extension and differentiation

● Clench the stick in the middle so that cubes are visible on both sides of your hand, then let the children estimate how many there are all together.

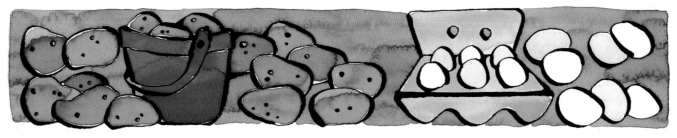

● Clench the stick at both ends so that several cubes are visible between your hands. Let the children estimate how many cubes there are.

● Use only one or two fingers to cover cubes.

The children took turns to conceal cubes in their hands.

● Use both of your hands clenched close together to hold a longer cube stick.

● Let the children take turns to hold the stick and hide the cubes.

## Ping pong balls

### Group size:
four to six children.

### You will need:
an egg box; six ping pong balls.

### The activity
Show the children the ping pong balls and the egg box and give them a chance to handle them if they wish. Count together the number of spaces in the egg box and make sure that the children know how many 'eggs' it will hold by counting the balls in and out of the box.

Ask the children to close their eyes. Put a few of the balls into the box and close the lid. Let the children have a 'quick peek' in the box by lifting the lid and very quickly replacing it. Ask the children how many balls they think are in the box. If they guess/estimate reasonably, allow them to count to check. Discuss which guesses were too high, too low, or very close.

### Extension and differentiation
● Let the children take turns at being 'in charge' and put the balls in the box for others to peek at.

● Increase the number of ping pong balls and use a 12-egg box.

● Let the children find their guesses and the actual number on a number line. Discuss how close or far away the guesses are.

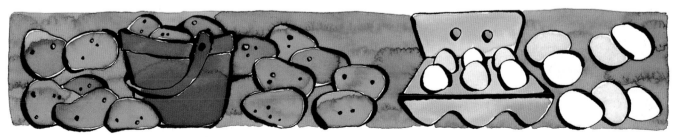

## Potatoes

### Group size:

four to six children.

### You will need:

several large potatoes; several small potatoes; a small seaside bucket.

### The activity

Ask the children to fill the bucket with large potatoes, then to estimate how many there are. Help them with suggestions ('Do you think there are more or fewer than ten? Five?'). Let the children count the potatoes to find out how many there are. Discuss whose estimate was greater or smaller than the actual number.

Now ask them to fill the bucket with small potatoes. Discuss whether there will be more than, fewer than or the same number as when it was filled with big ones. Ask the children how they know. Let them count how many small potatoes are in the bucket.

### Extension and differentiation

● Repeat the activity with bigger and smaller containers, and bigger and smaller objects, for example, stones in yoghurt pots, balls in bowls, conkers and acorns in cartons.

● Give the children number cards. Let them choose a card that they think represents the number of potatoes in any particular container, then compare it with the actual number. Ask them whether it is a higher or lower number.

## Assessment

Estimation is a difficult aspect of number to assess, but there are several points to bear in mind as you assess particular children.

● Are the children's estimates reasonable?

● Do the children understand that if they can only fit six balls in an egg box, any estimate above six is not reasonable?

● Can the children make estimates of numbers which are larger than they can count to, for example, more/fewer than 100, 50 or 20? (Their responses can give a good insight into their understanding of number.)

## Evidence of the children's learning

The children loved playing *Sticks* and often chose to play it on their own. They used phrases like 'It can't be…' and 'It's probably about…' when they were guessing, and sometimes contradicted each other.

They also played the same game with beads on a string. These were much smaller than the cubes. At first, the children's estimates were much lower than the actual number, so we discussed why this might be. Clare said that the beads must be bigger because the numbers were bigger, but Khywan said, 'No – they are smaller, to hide more,' which was an exciting breakthrough.

## Other quick ideas

● As often as possible, encourage the children to estimate before counting, for example, how many children are in the group, are here today, need a drink, and so on.

● Let the children decide how many pencils are needed. Ask them whether you need more or less than a handful.

● Have discussions about how many elephants they think would fit into the room, or lorries in the playground, fairies on their hand, cows in the play house, and so on. Encourage the children to explain how they arrive at their estimates. In this case the estimates cannot be checked, and hence cannot be right or wrong, but the reasoning process will support the children in their more realistic estimates.

● Have fun with the children discussing, for example, how many conkers could not fit in a container.

## Involving parents

Suggest various estimating activities that parents and children can try out at home together. For example, estimate how many stairs or steps there are at home, then check; estimate how many packets of biscuits, apples, tins of beans there are at home, then check; estimate how many times the word 'the' appears in the rhyme 'Humpty Dumpty', then sing it together a few times to check.

# Recognising and writing symbols

## Intended learning

To read and write numerals; to use number names; to begin to record by writing numerals.

## Introduction

The ability to recognise symbols, for example the symbol 3 as a representation of the spoken word 'three', is a matching skill, which has direct links with learning to read. As well as making the connection between what is heard and what is seen, children need to appreciate that any group of three items, whether large or small, is represented by the symbol 3. They should realise that it does not matter whether the symbol is large or small, or in another colour. Encourage them to consider what it is about the symbol 3 that characterises it.

These activities will help children to understand the meaning of number symbols. As their writing improves, the children will become proud of their ability to write them, especially the difficult ones like 5 and 8.

## Key vocabulary

**number names, shape, curve, straight line, top, bottom, back to front, side**

## Finger pencil

### Group size:
two to eight children.

### You will need:
a set of 0 to 9 number cards, with clearly written numerals, for each pair of children (or alternatively sets with just the numerals that the children are working on at the moment).

### The activity

Ask the children to work in pairs. Give each pair a set of cards and help them to decide which child in the pair is going to choose a number between one and nine. Explain that this number is to be kept a secret from the other child.

Show the child who chooses the number how to pretend that their finger is a pencil, and ask them to use their finger pencil to draw the numeral somewhere on the other child's body, such as on their hand or back. The second child should try to identify which numeral is being drawn and point to the correct card. Check that the children are writing the numbers correctly.

### Extension and differentiation

● If children have difficulty drawing the numerals, let them practise tracing over the number cards with their fingers.

● Hide the number card so that the child with the 'finger pencil' may not refer to it whilst drawing, and the second child has to say the number name rather than pointing to it.

# Feely bag

## Group size:
two to six children.

## You will need:
a bag; a set of numerals 0 to 5 cut from thick card or wood, with a textured material (such as sandpaper, fur or felt) stuck on the 'correct' side to aid identification.

## The activity
Place the numbers in the bag and shake them up. Let the children take it in turns to close their eyes and take out one of the numbers.

They should then feel the number carefully and try to guess which it is without being able to see it.

After a few children have had a turn, discuss with them how they decided which numeral they were holding.

## Extension and differentiation
● Reduce the number of numerals used as appropriate.

● Make two sets of numerals covered in different materials, such as felt and plastic. Put them in a 'feely bag', and ask the children to find pairs of numerals that are the same.

*Revealing the number from the 'feely bag'*

## Peep-bo

### Group size:
four to ten children.

### You will need:
a set of large numeral cards; a screen.

### The activity
Hold the cards behind a screen. Choose one and gradually reveal it bit by bit from behind the screen until the children are able to guess which number it is.

### Extension and differentiation
● Show the set of numeral cards to the children before the game and make sure they can identify each one.

● Let the children discuss all the possibilities at each stage. Make a list of the possibilities they identify.

● Let the children take turns to hide the number.

## Who am I?

### Group size:
four to six children.

### You will need:
a set of fairly large number cards (either 0 to 5 or 0 to 9).

### The activity
Place the number cards face up in front of the children. Describe one of the numbers to them (for example, 'I am a straight line from top to bottom'), and then ask 'Who am I?' Repeat the description if necessary and give the children a chance to suggest which number you have been describing. Hold up the correct number card and repeat your description. Then let the children take turns to choose a number and describe it.

### Extension and differentiation
● Before the game, trace each of the numbers with your finger, describing its shape as you do so.

● Repeat the game, but this time invite the children to write the numeral they think is being described.

## Assessment

● Can the children find one numeral among a group of others?

● Can they identify numbers when they are pointed to?

● Can children write all the single-digit numerals using the correct formation?

● If children cannot write the numerals, can they trace them? Can they trace them if you show them where to start? (It may be that the children cannot control a pencil, but they do know how to write the numerals.)

## Evidence of the children's learning

The children were particularly excited when we played *Peep-bo*. They quickly got better at being able to explain why the peeping shape could or could not be a particular number. It was also interesting to note the development of the language they used to describe the shape they saw – words and phrases like curved, straight, straight up and all the way round became commonplace during the game. They enjoyed playing so much that we made another version using pictures of common shapes.

## Other quick ideas

● Every day, write numbers 'in the air' and ask the children to copy you.

● Whenever children count, ask them to find the number on a number line.

● Display a large number line at the children's level so that they can get close to it and trace the numbers with their fingers.

● Make available a set of 'feely numbers' (for example, made from sandpaper), for the children to play with. The numbers could be displayed on the wall or in another prominent position in the room.

● Make deliberate mistakes when writing numerals for the children. Ask them to identify what is wrong. For example, the numeral 8 could be drawn with an extra 'ring' on it.

## Involving parents

Invite parents to participate in as many numeral-related activities as possible. For example, they could stick a number line on the refrigerator door for children to use for matching magnetic numbers; they could collect birthday cards with numbers on and let children stick them in a scrap book; they could help children to draw pages full of 2s, 3s, etc, of different sizes and in different colours.

# Tens

## Intended learning

To begin to know what each digit in a number represents; to count a collection of objects; to begin to count in tens; to begin to learn the names for larger numbers.

## Introduction

The activities in this section focus on groups of ten, the most important number in the decimal system. As soon as children can count beyond nine, they encounter two-digit numbers – the world of 'tens and units'. In later years, many of the problems children (and some adults) have with number are due to an insufficient understanding of the significance of ten.

## Key vocabulary

group, more, less, fewer, digit, least, most, fewest

## Threading

### Group size:

up to eight children.

### You will need:

beads or cotton reels; a long length of string for each child.

### The activity

Ask the children each to choose a colour and then find ten beads or reels of that colour. Invite them to thread them on to the string. Then let them choose another colour, and continue threading until there are enough beads or reels on the string to match their height. Discuss the children's strings with them: 'How many tens are there?' 'Did you need to add on a few extra beads or reels in order to match your height?'

### Extension and differentiation

● Encourage the children to count as they thread the beads or reels.

● Use shorter lengths of string and let the children thread just one group of ten on to each one.

● Ask the children to make threaded strings of different lengths, for example to match the height of the door, the height of the teacher or the distance around the play house.

● Invite the children to work in pairs. Ask one child in each pair to thread beads on to a length of string to match the other child's height.

● Work together as a group to match the distance across, or around, the whole room.

● Discuss how many beads there might be all together in the threaded lengths of string.

# Hedgehogs

## Group size:
four to six children.

## You will need:
a dice; Plasticine; lolly sticks or headless matchsticks; a shoe box for each child.

## The activity
Give each child a large lump of Plasticine and a shoe box, then explain that they are going to make hedgehog nests.

Let the children take turns to roll the dice and collect that number of sticks. When they have collected ten sticks, let them use Plasticine to make a round hedgehog body and push the sticks in to make spines. Then let them place their hedgehog in its shoe box nest. Any left-over matchsticks should be put aside to make the next hedgehog.

After, say, four rounds, the player with the most complete hedgehogs in their nest wins the game. It is possible that some children might not have collected enough sticks to make even one hedgehog, so they may need to continue the game for one or two more rounds.

## Extension and differentiation
● Use a 1, 2, 3, 1, 2, 3 dice. The first player to make one hedgehog is the winner.

● Change the rules so that it is the first person with three (or any other appropriate number) hedgehogs in their nest who wins the game.

Throwing the dice to collect spines for the hedgehogs

## Yoghurt pots

### Group size:

up to six children.

### You will need:

a tray of conkers (or shells, stones or beads); empty yoghurt pots; a dice.

### The activity

Ask the children to take turns to roll the dice, say the number shown and collect that number of conkers. The first player to collect ten (or more) puts them in a yoghurt pot and wins the game.

### Extension and differentiation

● If necessary, let the children use a 1, 2, 3, 1, 2, 3 dice.

● Provide the children with a tray containing a mixture of objects. Ask them to repeat the game, with each child collecting specific items.

● Extend the game so that the winner is the first person to collect two yoghurt pots containing ten conkers.

## Tens

### Group size:
three to ten children.

### You will need:
a wide range of items, including at least ten examples of each item.

### The activity
Ask the children to collect ten of anything! This could include, for example, ten grains of rice, ten pencils, ten pieces of paper, ten children, ten chairs, ten leaves, ten flowers, and so on. Ask the children questions about their collections ('Which take up the most space?' 'Which ones could you fit in your pocket?' 'Which take up the least space?').

### Extension and differentiation
● Let the children work in pairs. Ask them to collect specific items that have an obvious contrast in size, such as ten beads and ten books. Ask them similar questions to those in the main activity.

● Ask the children what ten things they could collect to fill a particular container, such as a bucket, a thimble or a pocket.

## Assessment

● Can the children consistently group in tens?

● Can children count in tens and respond to questions such as 'How many sticks did you need to make your three hedgehogs?' without attempting to count individual sticks?

## Evidence of the children's learning

It was in the game of *Hedgehogs* that the children's learning was most evident. After two games where only one hedgehog was required to win, the children were asked how we could make the game last longer. Someone volunteered the idea that the winner should have to make two hedgehogs – 'Then they wouldn't be on their own in the nest.' The children played this way until there was a winner who commented, 'Ten and ten – that's twenty.' This had not been the objective of the activity, but it was an exciting outcome.

## Other quick ideas

● Arrange the children in groups of ten and ask them to work out from the number of groups how many children there are in the class all together.

● Let the children take turns to roll a dice and collect the appropriate number of pennies. The first player with ten pennies wins the game.

● Store pencils, pens and other items of equipment in groups of ten. Draw the children's attention to this when getting out or putting away the equipment.

## Involving parents

Ask parents to let their children sort pennies into piles of ten, then swap them for the appropriate number of 10p coins. They could also work together to find groups of ten things at home (toy cars, teddies or spoons), or try to walk across one of the rooms at home in exactly ten steps.

# Sorting

## Intended learning

To sort objects by one criterion; to collect, record and discuss data; to begin to record by writing numerals; to begin to count a collection of objects reliably; to begin to read numerals.

## Introduction

The activities in this unit introduce the concept of using criteria to sort objects and to draw Venn and Carroll diagrams. The same basic information can be recorded on both types of diagram. These activities focus on sorting by only one criterion. At this level, single-criterion sorting will be sufficient for the children to work with. There may, however, be some children who are ready to sort by two criteria, for example colour and shape, and can extend the diagrammatic representations accordingly.

Any of the following types of items can be used for these sorting activities, although the questions will, of course, need to be reworded accordingly: shoes, boxes, pegs, buttons, cars, stickers, toys, lids, socks, stones, ribbons, hats, birthday cards, shells.

## Key vocabulary

**diagram, more, less, most, fewer, fewest, direction, rule**

Venn diagram

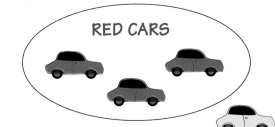

Carroll diagram

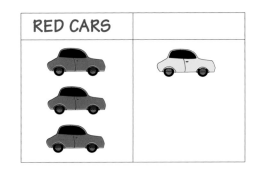

## Who can find?

### Group size:

three to eight children.

### You will need:

a box containing items for sorting.

### The activity

Ask the children to sort through the box to find items with a specific feature (for example, something with red on it). Ask them to put the items back, then offer them another criterion (for example, something with wheels).

### Extension and differentiation

● Restrict the items in the box to a limited number of patterns, colours, etc.

● Ask the children to find an item that fulfils two criteria at once.

● Let the children take turns to choose the criteria.

# Sorting cards

## Group size:
at least ten children.

## You will need:
a collection of old birthday cards (or other items suitable for sorting); a large drawing of a blank Venn diagram on a big piece of paper (or simply use a PE hoop); marker pen.

## The activity
Allow each child to choose a birthday card that they particularly like. Discuss the pictures on the cards with the children ('Are there any with animals on? What are the animals?' 'Are there any with buildings on? What sort of buildings?' 'Are there any with pink on? What other colours are there?' 'What else can you notice about your pictures?').

Agree on one particular criterion for sorting, such as pictures of birds. Explain to the children that on your Venn diagram, all the cards with pictures of birds belong inside the set. Let the children watch as you write a label for the set. Ask them in turn to place their card either inside or outside the set, depending on whether or not it has a bird on it. When all the cards have been placed on the diagram, discuss the outcomes with the children: 'How many cards are on the diagram?' 'How many cards with a bird picture are there?' 'How many cards without a bird picture are there?' 'Are there more cards inside or outside the set?'

Birthday cards offer a variety of potential criteria for sorting.

This activity is ideal for working either with two groups simultaneously or with one group after another. Both groups can then join together to discuss and compare the resulting Venn diagrams. This gives the children an opportunity to interpret a diagram that they have not made themselves, and will enhance their understanding of the diagrams.

## Extension and differentiation

● Support the children by asking questions as they sort ('How are you sorting the objects?' 'Why does this one go in there?' 'Why doesn't this one go in there?').

● Let the children work with two criteria, such as cards with pictures of birds and cards with pictures of flowers. Can they find any cards that belong in both sets?

# What's in my pocket?

## Group size:
two to eight children.

## You will need:
a small everyday object, such as a pencil, counter or bead.

## The activity
Place a simple item such as a pencil in your pocket. Challenge the children to try to identify what is hidden in your pocket by asking you questions to which you may only answer 'Yes' or 'No'. (You may need to help them to rephrase their questions. For example, 'Has it got legs?' may be asked, but not 'How many legs has it got?') From time to time remind the children of what they have discovered so far. When you think they have enough information, give them a chance to guess what the object is.

## Extension and differentiation

● If the children find it difficult to decide what to ask, give them prompts such as 'Ask me something about what it's used for' or 'Ask me about its shape.' You may need to spend some time talking about what kind of questions might be useful.

● Allow one of the children to have a turn at hiding something. This often works better if you provide some kind of screen so that the child can look at the object as an aid to answering the questions.

# Guess game

## Group size:
eight to 16 children.

## You will need:
chalk; floor space.

## The activity
Draw a chalk line on the floor. On one side write 'yes' and on the other side write 'no'.

Decide on a criterion connected with what the children are wearing (for example, wearing trainers), but don't tell them what it is. Ask each child in turn to stand on either the 'yes' side or the 'no' side, depending on whether or not they match your criterion. Once all the children have been placed, invite them to try to guess what the criterion is.

## Extension and differentiation

● If necessary, support the children by giving them clues ('It's about what you are wearing.' 'There is something the same about all the people in the 'yes' section.' 'Look at your feet.')

● When the children understand the game, try using other sorting items, for example a box of buttons, and using criteria like 'buttons with four holes' or 'shiny buttons'. This works better with a desk-sized sorting diagram, rather than one on the floor.

● Choose one child to whisper their own idea for a criterion to you, and to place the appropriate items on the correct side of the line. Again, the whole group must try to guess the rule.

● When children are confident with the concept of items on the 'yes' side having a common attribute, discuss what it is that is the same about all the things on the 'no' side (the only thing they have in common is that they do not have the chosen attribute).

## Assessment

● Can the children sort items consistently?

● Can they can sort items on to the diagrams described here?

● Can children interpret the information shown on a sorting diagram?

● Can they say what the diagram is about? Can they say what it tells us?

## Evidence of the children's learning

The *Guess game* was an activity that the children found challenging at first, and they needed plenty of clues about what to look for. They found it difficult to make use of the 'no' set when trying to find the attribute common to all the 'yes' children. After several tries, however, the children began to ask for the clues themselves ('Is it about what they are wearing?' 'Is it to do with colours?'), which was a useful step.

## Other quick ideas

● Use stories as a source of data. Choose a book each and count the number of children, birds, cars, and so on, in each book.

● Make links with measurement by sorting the children according to how tall they are, how far they can throw a ball, how many cubes they can hold in their hand, and so on.

● Sort the children according to how many buttons they have on their clothing, whether or not they are wearing a cardigan, and so on.

## Involving parents

Ask parents to encourage their children to sort as many different items as possible at home – cutlery, clothes, toys, jewellery, playing cards, etc. Children could also be allowed to help put the shopping away in the right places.

# Pattern

## Intended learning

To recognise, copy and extend simple patterns; to make simple patterns.

## Introduction

The word 'pattern' is one that has a more specific meaning in mathematics than it often does in everyday language, where it can be used to mean a design or arrangement. In mathematics, a pattern can be represented in a number of ways, for example, ABABABAB, XYXYXYXY and 12121212 are essentially the same pattern.

These activities support children's developing understanding until they can appreciate the 'sameness' of patterns. There are several stages in this development process. The first stage is when children can recognise and copy a given pattern. A deeper level of understanding is demonstrated when children can continue a pattern they have been given. True under-standing of pattern is illustrated when children can devise their own pattern, and can explain why it is a pattern (usually because there is a repeated unit), and later can identify the sameness of patterns.

## Key vocabulary

**before, after, next, again,**

**repeat, the same, in front,**

**behind, after, similar**

## Pattern in my pocket

### Group size:

four to eight children.

### You will need:

a pre-prepared strip of squared paper coloured in a pattern sequence, such as the one shown below.

### The activity

Show the strip of paper to the children and let them call out the sequence of colours as you point to the squares. Discuss with them what would come next if the paper had been longer.

Put the strip of paper in your pocket and carefully pull it out, one coloured square at a time. Ask the children to try to guess which colour comes next before each new square emerges from your pocket.

### Extension and differentiation

● If children are struggling with predicting the pattern, restrict it to two colours (for example, red, blue, red, blue).

● Support children by using equipment that they can touch, such as beads on a string, or coloured paperclips fixed together. Recite the colour sequence out loud with them.

● Do not show the pattern to the children in advance. This ensures that they must recognise the pattern, rather than just remember it.

● Try more complex patterns, or let the children make up the patterns.

The children's understanding of pattern was developed by passing a ball in a repeated sequence.

## Pass the ball

### Group size:
eight to 16 children.

### You will need:
a large ball.

### The activity
Ask the children to stand in a line one behind the other with a small space in between.

Give the ball to the child at the front and explain that they are going to pass the ball from the front of the line to the back. Let the children practise passing the ball along the line from hand to hand.

When the children are confident with this, explain that they now have to concentrate hard because they are going to pass the ball in a pattern. Suggest that the first child passes the ball through their legs, the next passes it over their head, the next through their legs, and so on until the end of the line is reached.

After a few practices, let the children try to say the pattern at the same time ('under, over, under, over, under...'), making sure that the words match the actions. After a few more practices, encourage them to try to speed up!

Finally, try inventing some different ways of passing, such as under the arm or twisting to the right or to the left to pass the ball.

## Extension and differentiation

● Support children by talking about the pattern that is being made ('If Amy is passing the ball over her head, which way will Geeta pass it next?').

● Let the children have a race in two teams.

● Extend the game so that when the ball reaches the last child, he or she runs with it to the front of the line to continue the pattern.

● Ask the children to find a way to record the game on paper.

# Movement patterns

## Group size:
ten or more children.

## You will need:
a large space such as the hall or playground; a drum or a tambourine.

## The activity
Explore patterns in movement by asking the children to move in simple repeated sequences in time to the sounds of your drumbeat or tambourine. For example, to a slow single beat, ask them to stand on the spot and touch the top of their head with both hands, then touch their toes, head, toes, head, toes, and so on.

To one slow and two fast beats, ask them to move around the room doing one jump, two hops, one jump, two hops, and so on.

## Extension and differentiation
● Support children by using a slow single beat and just two very simple movements.

● Ask the children to match movements to different sounds. For example, when you tap the tambourine, the children should jump, and when you shake it, they should wiggle. Play the sounds in a repeated sequence so that the children are doing a pattern of movements, and hence have the opportunity to predict the next movement.

# Assessment

● Can the children copy a simple repeating ABABA pattern?

● Can they extend it?

● Can the children copy a simple ABABA pattern of cubes, but using different colours? (For example, 'Make the same pattern as my red and blue one, but use yellow and green cubes.') Can they explain how they know that their pattern is the same as yours?

● Can they make a similar pattern using a different kind of equipment (for example, triangle, square, triangle, square)?

● Can they make new patterns of their own? (This is often where children have difficulty. Their understanding can be supported by discussing what a pattern is – something that repeats.) What do the children think a pattern is?

● Can the children make more complex patterns (AABAABAAB, and so on)?

# Evidence of the children's learning

The children loved all these games, and many of them could immediately recognise a pattern of single repeats in a number of contexts. They were often unwilling to stop their pattern in the *Movement patterns* activity.

More complex patterns (such as 122122 or 123123) were recognised by some of the children in a visual context, such as in *Pattern in my pocket*, and they were very pleased with themselves when they could predict what colour would emerge next – although some continued to expect a single repeat.

Stacey was not only able to recognise a more complex pattern, but she also generated some intricate ones of her own on a pegboard as a follow-up to this work. She was able to identify errors when two pegs were swapped around.

# Other quick ideas

● Find patterns in the room (desk, chair, desk, chair) or patterns in the displays (picture, name, picture, name).

● Look for patterns outside the school (window, window, door, window, window, door, window, window, door, in a block of flats; patterns in brickwork; patterns in flowerbeds in gardens).

● Sit the children in a circle and say a pattern around the group. The first child says 'yes,' the second says 'no,' the next says 'yes,' and so on. Try other spoken patterns (yes, yes, no, yes, yes, no; or cup, saucer, cup, saucer).

# Involving parents

Ask parents to help their children find patterns on the fabric of clothes or on carpets, wallpaper or bedspreads. Children could be allowed to copy the patterns on paper using paint or felt-tipped pens. Children could also make patterns with cutlery (fork, spoon, fork, spoon, fork), and listen for patterns in sounds, such as the ding-dong ding-dong of a chiming clock, or the brrr-brrr brrr-brrr of a telephone.

# Odds and evens

## Intended learning

To begin to recognise odd and even numbers; to count rhythmically in twos; to develop a sense of 'odd' and 'even'.

## Introduction

These activities aim to introduce children to the idea that even numbers can be grouped into twos with no spares, and odd numbers cannot. Only whole numbers are even or odd. Zero/0 is a special number/symbol and the children should recognise it as such. Children can often recite/say the even numbers, but struggle with the odd numbers so it is important to give equal attention to both throughout all the following activities.

## Key vocabulary

group, more, less, fewer, equal, same, spare, left over, odd, even

## Cubes game

### Group size:

two to eight children.

### You will need:

interlocking cubes.

### The activity

The children can either play this game in pairs, or as two groups.

Invite each child, or one child from each group, to take a handful of cubes. Ask them both to try to make two sticks of equal length. If they can do so using all their cubes, they 'win'. Explain that if there is a cube left over when they try to make two sticks the same length, they have not won. Lead them to understand that they only win if they pick up an even number of cubes.

Children rarely know the words 'odd' and 'even', but with enough discussion can come to understand that the odd numbers are those which leave a spare cube when they are divided into two equal groups.

### Extension and differentiation

● Encourage the children to count their cubes before they make them into sticks. Can they predict whether or not they can make two sticks of equal length? Discuss with the children which are 'good' and which are 'bad' numbers to pick up, and ask them how they know. Encourage the answer that even numbers make 'winning' towers, but odd numbers do not.

● Introduce a set of number cards 1 to 10 (or 1 to 20, depending on the children's ability). Ask each child or group in turn to choose a number card and then collect that

number of cubes with which to try to make two equal sticks. Ask the children to mark on their number card whether it was a 'good' or a 'bad' number to choose. For example, they could mark the cards with smiley or sad faces, ticks or crosses, or just write on 'yes' or 'no'. After most of the cards have been marked (which may not happen during one game), let the children put the number cards in order and look for a pattern of good and bad numbers. The numbers should show the odd/even/odd/even pattern.

● Introduce and encourage children to use the terms 'odd' and 'even' throughout.

## Socks

### Group size:
four to ten children.

### You will need:
a collection of pairs of socks (preferably real ones, but the activity will still work with paper or card pictures of socks); a bag; clothes pegs; a length of string suspended at child height to act as a washing-line.

### The activity
Divide the children into two teams and ask them to stand at either end of the washing-line. Place the bag of socks in the middle. Ask the teams to take turns to send one child to pick out two socks from the bag without looking. Explain that if they pick out a matching pair of socks they can take them back to their

Sorting socks into pairs to see if there is an odd or even amount

end of the washing-line and peg them up. If not, they must put the socks back in the bag. The winning team is the one with the most pairs on the line when the bag is empty.

Discuss how many pairs of socks each team has, and how many socks they have all together. Emphasise that numbers that can be made into pairs are 'even' numbers.

## Extension and differentiation

● Use only three or four pairs of socks.

● Support children by letting them sort a bag of socks into pairs. Stress the fact that even numbers make pairs. If there is a sock left over, then there is an odd number of socks.

● Give the game more variety by putting pairs of socks and pairs of gloves in the bag.

## Whisper counts

### Group size:
four to ten children.

### You will need:
no special equipment.

### The activity
Introduce the activity by asking the children to count together to a given number according to their ability. Ask them to count out loud and then count again in a whisper.

Once it is clear that the children are fairly secure in counting to the number you have given them, ask them to join in with you and count once more, alternating between a loud voice and a whisper as they say the numbers. They can whisper the odd numbers and say the even numbers out loud, or vice versa.

## Extension and differentiation

● Reinforce the concept of odd and even by asking the children questions about the game: 'If we start counting with a whisper at one, what number will be the next one that we whisper?' 'What about the next whispered number after that?' 'Can anyone say just the whispered numbers? Just the out loud numbers?' 'If we start with a whisper at one, will we say or whisper number nine?'

● Sit the children in a circle and ask them to count round the group, alternating between saying their number out loud and whispering.

● Ask the children to try counting backwards. Once they can do this, invite them to try alternating between whispering and speaking out loud as before.

● Start counting from a different number, such as five.

## Assessment

● Do the children know and understand the words 'odd' and 'even'? (The children could be asked directly if they know what it means if a number is odd or even. This question requires them to make a general statement, which is a sophisticated idea and it is unusual for children of this age to be able to articulate with accuracy. However, after trying these activities some children will be able to explain. Note that there will be some children who will have memorised which numbers are odd/even. This, however, does not truly reflect understanding.)

● Do they understand what odd-ness and even-ness are, even if they do not know the words? (Children will often use a strategy without being able to explain, or even identify it.)

## Evidence of the children's learning

The children particularly liked the *Socks* game and many chose to put pairs of socks on the line in their own free time. The development of language was particularly noticeable when they described what they were doing. They used the words 'pairs' and 'odd socks' comfortably and with understanding.

We developed the game by putting more than two socks of the same type in the bag. The children counted the socks and hung them on the line in pairs. They began to be able to predict which numbers of socks they would and would not be able to hang up in pairs.

## Other quick ideas

● Every day, ask the children to get into pairs. Then discuss whether there is an odd or even number of children present.

● Give the children toy animals. Invite them to line them up two by two to go into the ark. Is there an odd or even number of animals?

● Sing 'Ten fat sausages', using Plasticine sausages as props. Change the number of sausages, so that instead of always counting back in twos from ten they start from, say, seven. Which numbers of sausages mean that there isn't a sausage left to bang at the end?

## Involving parents

Ask parents to let their children practise pairing socks, gloves and shoes. Children could also sort cutlery into sets of knife and fork, or spoon and fork, or sort a pot of pennies into twos, and then swap two pennies for a 2p coin.

# Recognising errors

## Intended learning

To recite the number names in order to ten; to recite the number names in order counting on from a given number; to recite the number names in order counting back from a given number; to recognise and make simple repeating patterns; to begin to check their work and identify errors.

## Introduction

To be able to identify mistakes and absurdities in mathematics at this level helps children to reflect on their answers and judge whether or not they are correct. Many children believe that finding an error in their work is a bad thing. They need to be led to understand that part of the process of learning and doing is stopping and taking stock every now and then. The ability to identify errors is both essential and a good thing to practise. As teachers we need to praise children's ability to do this.

The activities in this section are about giving children the confidence and the opportunity to look for and to find errors. There is also scope in activities in other units to make 'deliberate mistakes' for the children to spot.

## Key vocabulary

number names, start, finish, different, next, last, repeat, missing, wrong, order, pattern, space

## Missing

### Group size:
four to 16 children.

### You will need:
no special equipment.

### The activity

Introduce the activity by counting with the whole group. Develop this by asking the children to stop at a particular number. You might say, for example, 'I want you to start at one but remember to stop when you get to six.' This usually needs a few tries before everyone gets the idea! Then extend this further by asking the children to start and stop at particular numbers. For example, 'This time start at three and stop at eight.' This is much more difficult, as the children now have two things to remember.

Now suggest to the children that you are getting a bit forgetful, and ask them to help you by spotting what you are forgetting when you try counting. Count out loud from one to ten, but miss out one number near the middle. Can the children tell you what was wrong? The sequence may need to be repeated.

### Extension and differentiation

● If the children find identifying the missing number difficult, make it more obvious by pausing or nodding when you reach the position where it should be in the sequence.

● Give each child a set of 1 to 10 number cards. Repeat the activity but this time, instead of telling you the missing number, the children should find the correct number card and hold it up to show you.

● Use sequences that do not begin at one, for example, three, four, five, seven, eight, nine. Children find this particularly tricky, as it is much more difficult than the earlier activities, but they will often succeed. They may respond that one and two are the missing numbers. Emphasise that your sequence begins at three, so they need to find something else that is missing.

● Try saying the sequences in reverse from highest to lowest.

*The children were able to rearrange number cards and peg them on a line in the right order.*

## Pegs

### Group size:
four to eight children.

### You will need:
a length of string or a skipping rope suspended between two chairs; clothes pegs; a set of 0 to 3 number cards.

### The activity
Peg the number cards on to the washing-line in the wrong order. Ask the children what is wrong, then let them sort the numbers and peg them up in the right order. It is not essential that the sequences run from left to right (pegging up 3 2 1 0 would be acceptable), but they should be read out from left to right.

## Extension and differentiation

● Children who are struggling with the activity can be helped to focus on the numbers (rather than the colours of the pegs, for example) by saying the numbers out loud in the order they appear on the line and being reminded of the proper sequence.

● Children can also be supported by being allowed to refer to a number line.

● Increase the range of the number cards.

● Let one of the children peg up the numbers in the wrong order, then ask the rest of the group to rearrange them correctly.

● Change the activity by pegging up simple number patterns (instead of numbers for counting) for the children to find and correct any missing numbers or to remove any 'extra' numbers (for example, 1 2 1 2 1 2 1 2 2 1 2 1 2 and 2 4 2 4 3 2 4 2 4 2).

● Use a set of numbers that are not sequential, such as 2 5 6 8, and peg them up in the wrong order. Can the children put them in order? Can they tell you which numbers are missing?

# Animal patterns

## Group size:

four to six children.

## You will need:

sets of toy animals, such as farm animals, zoo animals or dinosaurs.

## The activity

Introduce the activity by showing the children two groups of animals with at least five of the same animal in each set, for example: five sheep and five cows; six lions and six zebras; or five tyrannosaurus rex and five brontosaurus. Arrange the two sets of toys in front of the children in a simple repeating pattern, for example: sheep, cow, sheep, cow, sheep, cow, sheep, cow, sheep, cow.

Give the children an opportunity to look at and talk about the pattern you have made ('Which animal would come next? And after that?' 'How do you know?'). Point to the animals one by one from left to right and ask the children to say their names. Emphasise the pattern.

Explain that you are going to play a game. Ask the children to close their eyes, then either add an extra animal in the middle of the row or take one away. Let the children open their eyes and ask them what is wrong with the animal pattern now.

## Extension and differentiation

● If the children find this difficult, let them say the names of the animals as you point to them again. This may help them to spot the missing or extra animal.

● Extend the activity by making the animal patterns more complex.

● Let the children take turns to add or take away an animal to upset the pattern.

## Assessment

● Are the children able to spot errors in a range of situations?

● Are they able to explain why a number sequence or pattern is wrong?

● Are they able to say how an error can be put right?

## Evidence of the children's learning

The children loved spotting errors. Looking for 'deliberate mistakes' – which might occur at any time – soon became part of everyday life. As time passed, the playing of these games made the children less fearful of making mistakes. On occasions they were able to spot their own errors (in counting, for example) and even pretended that they were making a deliberate mistake for the others to spot!

The children particularly enjoyed *Pegs* and they soon began to work with numbers up to at least five. It was helpful for them to use the number line on the wall at first, but eventually they were able to manage without it.

## Other quick ideas

● Show the children a number card, then make a tower of cubes with the wrong number of cubes in it. Can the children put it right?

● Draw pictures with obvious errors for the children to find, such as a person with two heads!

● When handing out pencils, paintbrushes, drinks, and so on, give two to one child 'by mistake'. You could turn this into a daily joke.

● Put the wrong number of pieces of paper (pencils, books, and so on) on the table for the children. Ask them to explain what is wrong and how it needs to be corrected.

## Involving parents

Encourage the children to play tricks on their parents as you have being doing with them, making sure you have warned parents about this game in advance! Suitable tricks could include getting out one too many spoons and asking the parent to say what is wrong. When playing counting games, parents and children could take turns to make 'deliberate mistakes' and challenge each other to say what they are.

# Addition

## Intended learning

To count on from a given number; to begin to understand and use the vocabulary of addition; to begin to understand addition as the combination of two groups; to begin to understand addition as counting on; to separate a number of objects into two groups; to add one to a number.

## Introduction

Children develop a feeling for addition (and subtraction) without either the need or the ability to record their calculations. Writing out equations, such as $6 + 2 = 8$, is a way of recording addition, but on its own rarely leads children directly to an understanding of the concept. Much groundwork should be done before children meet this way of writing down calculations. This groundwork should focus on the breadth of language associated with addition, for example, add, more, count on, equals, and so on. These activities do not involve recording addition, but are intended to help children towards an understanding of addition as the joining of two or more groups, or as the expansion of one.

## Key vocabulary

count, count on, add, addition, equals, together, all together, group, more, plus, and, makes

## Fingers

### Group size:
two to 16 children.

### You will need:
no special equipment.

### The activity

Introduce the activity by asking all the children to sit on one of their hands, and to show you the fingers on their other hand and count them one at a time. Then ask them to show you two fingers on that hand. Encourage them to find as many ways as they can of holding up two fingers on one hand. Invite some of the children to come out to the front to show all the different ways that have been found. Repeat the activity using other numbers.

### Extension and differentiation

● Support children by counting 'one, two' as the fingers are held up. Help them to understand that however the fingers are held up, there are still two of them.

● Ask the children to hold up four fingers using two hands. Encourage them to find as many different ways of doing this as they can. Repeat with other numbers.

● Collect all the ways of showing a given number and make a display. The children could draw round their hands and cut out the drawings, then fingers could be cut off to make the required number.

The children were able to make specific numbers with their fingers.

# Dancing fingers

## Group size:
four to 12 children.

## You will need:
one paper plate for each pair of children; marker pen; taped music.

## The activity
Write a number between 0 and 5 on each plate. Ask the children to form pairs. Each pair should choose a plate and sit facing each other with the plate on the floor between them. Play the music and ask the children to make all their fingers 'dance' to it. Explain that when the music stops the children must place a number of fingers on their plate. However, they must make up the correct number of fingers between them – not each!

When the children are confident with this, let them swap plates with other pairs and try other numbers.

Note: zero seldom causes a problem for children in this context, and they usually invent a way to show it. These often illustrate children's understanding of zero, such as a clenched fist held near the plate.

## Extension and differentiation
● If the children find this difficult, try using only the numerals 1 to 3.

● Spread the plates out around the floor. When the music plays, ask the whole group to dance between the plates. When the music stops, encourage the children to go to the nearest plate. The children round a particular plate must work together to place the correct number of fingers on the plate.

## Frogs

### Group size:

two to six children.

### You will need:

large sheets of green paper; scissors; a big dice.

### The activity

Cut out approximately ten lily pad shapes, large enough for a child to stand on, from green paper. Arrange the lily pads in a wavy line across the floor, with sufficient space between them for children to be able to jump easily from pad to pad.

Introduce the activity by asking one child to pretend be a frog. Ask the child to stand on the first lily pad, then to roll the dice.

Explain that the frog is going to hop along as many lily pads as is shown on the dice. Encourage all the children to discuss where the frog will end up, then let the frog hop along to check. Let the frog roll the dice again until it can hop off the end of the line of lily pads.

Let each child take a turn at being the frog.

### Extension and differentiation

● Use a 1, 2, 3, 1, 2, 3 dice if the children are having difficulty with the addition sums.

● Make two lines of lily pads, appoint two frogs, and let them take turns at rolling the dice and predicting where they will get to. The first frog to reach the end of their line of lily pads wins the game.

● Number the lily pads and ask the frogs which number lily pad they think they will get to after their hops.

## Assessment

● Are the children showing signs of beginning to understand addition?

● Can they demonstrate and tell you three different ways of showing five fingers using both hands?

● Can they predict some of the outcomes in the numbered version of *Frogs*?

## Evidence of the children's learning

*Dancing fingers* was a favourite activity. Several children reached the point where they could offer two or three responses to questions such as 'Is there another way you could have put four fingers on there?' Daria was able to identify all the different ways of making four.

## Other quick ideas

● Play 'One more'. Give the children a number, or show them a number of cubes, then ask them to say the number which is one more. Try 'Two more', and so on.

● Let one child show a certain number of fingers on one hand, for example three. Ask all the children to count them together. Then ask another child to hold up enough extra fingers to make, say, six fingers all together.

● Play 'Steps' by asking two to six children to stand at one side of the room. Let other children roll a dice for each of them in turn, to determine the number of steps they may take. The first across the room wins the game.

● Do 'Children sums' by rolling a dice, then asking the appropriate number of children to stand at one side of the room. Roll again, then ask that number of children to stand on the other side of the room. Ask the rest of the group to work out how many children there will be if the two groups stand together.

## Involving parents

Ask parents to play 'I'm thinking of a number' with their children, for example, 'I'm thinking of a number. If I had two more, I would have five. What is my number?' Encourage parents to ask addition questions in everyday contexts, such as, 'How many different ways can five apples be arranged in two bowls?'

# Subtraction

## Intended learning

To count back from a given number; to begin to understand and use the vocabulary of subtraction; to subtract one number from another in a 'real life context'; to remove a smaller number from a larger and count the remainder; to solve simple problems in a 'real life context'; to make decisions.

## Introduction

Children come into contact with a variety of language associated with subtraction (minus, take away, difference, count back, fewer, etc). The word subtract encompasses all of them. Confusion can arise for children when the minus symbol is only called 'take away'. The activities in this unit cover the two different circumstances for which subtraction is the appropriate operation to use. The first is that of 'take away' ('There are six sweets and four are taken away – how many are left?'). The second is finding the difference ('You have six sweets and I have four – what is the difference?').

## Key vocabulary

count, count back, subtract, subtraction, equals, left, take away, difference, fewer

## Before

### Group size:
four to eight children.

### You will need:
no special equipment.

### The activity

Use sequences of actions to focus the children on the concept of looking back. Perform an example for them, such as: hands on head, touch nose, pat tummy, lift bent knee. Then let the children try to repeat the sequence. Discuss with the children what was the last thing they did, and before that, and so on. Then ask the children to perform the sequence backwards.

Repeat the activity, but this time ask the children to repeat the sequence backwards without any discussion.

### Extension and differentiation

● Reduce the number of actions in the sequence if children appear to be finding the game difficult.

● Ask the children to make up a sequence of two or three actions for the rest of the group to reverse.

● Make different kinds of sequences for the children to try to reverse, for example: sounds, such as clap, click, whistle, hum; things the children can see, such as shapes laid down in a sequence; story boards showing, for example, the process of getting dressed.

# Robbers

## Group size:
four to six children.

## You will need:
five pennies; a simple outline drawing of a pig.

## The activity
Introduce the activity by putting the pennies on the pig and letting all the children count them. Explain to the children that the pig represents a piggy bank for keeping the pennies safe.

Tell the children that you are going to pretend to be a robber. Ask the children to close their eyes (and cover them if keeping them closed is difficult!), then secretly take away some, or all, of the pennies on the pig. Ask the children to open their eyes, and let them look in horror at what the robber has done! Explain that the robber promises to return all the money if the children can say how many pennies have been taken. Let them offer suggestions as to how much has been taken. Discuss with the children how they worked out the answer. Did they guess? Did they use their fingers to help them?

Repeat the activity, letting one of the children be the robber.

## Extension and differentiation
● Use more or fewer pennies, depending on the children's abilities.

● Ask the children to find a way to record what happened. They will probably draw a picture or a diagram.

*The game of Robbers was an enjoyable introduction to subtraction.*

## Act it out

### Group size:
two to 16 children, or even more!

### You will need:
toys such as teddies and dolls (optional).

### The activity
Ask the whole group to sing together and act out such songs as 'There were ten in the bed' and 'Five currant buns'. Let the children suggest ways of acting the songs. For example, five children could be chosen to represent the currant buns, one child to be the shopkeeper and another the little boy. The actions might be as follows.

**Five currant buns in the baker's shop**
*(The five children stand in a line.)*
**Round and fat with sugar on the top**
*(They make themselves look fat
and pat their heads.)*
**Along came a boy with a penny one day**
*(The boy walks up to the five children.)*
**Bought a currant bun and took it away.**
*(The boy mimes paying the shopkeeper and
leads one of the five children away.)*

Alternatively, the children might prefer to use toys to act out the rhymes.

### Extension and differentiation
● Children who are struggling with the concept of subtraction can be helped by using a wide range of such action rhymes as frequently as possible.

● Try subtracting in twos by singing together 'Ten fat sausages'.

## Take one, take two

### Group size:
two to eight children.

### You will need:
several counters.

### The activity
Introduce this game by letting all the children form one team, with yourself as the other team.

Place a small pile of up to ten counters between you and the children. Explain that you are going to take one or two counters from the pile, then the children will have a turn at sending someone from their team to take away another one or two counters. This will continue until all the counters have been taken. Whoever takes the last one or two wins the game.

Play the game a few times in this way, then let the children play against each other in twos or threes.

### Extension and differentiation
● Ask the children to count the counters before they start, and then to count how many are left after each turn. Use this to reinforce the idea of subtraction as taking away.

● If appropriate to the children's abilities, let them take away up to three counters at a time.

## Assessment

● Do the children understand the concept of 'before' when sequencing actions?

● Can they say how many pennies would be left if the robber took three?

● Can children say how many counters will be left if you take one away? Two away?

## Evidence of the children's learning

During the *Robbers* game, children developed fascinating strategies for trying to decide how many pennies had been taken. None of them found their strategy particularly easy to explain, but with help, the following methods were identified. Some children just memorised (or attempted to memorise) where the coins had been, and made comments such as, 'Well there was one there and one there before, so the robber took two.' Some counted on from the number of coins that were left behind. Two children actually counted back from the number of coins that had been on the pig originally. This was a great activity for understanding children's thinking – even for those who just guessed every time.

## Other quick ideas

● Play 'Hide fingers'. Hold up one hand with all your fingers extended and count them together. Ask the children to close their eyes while you hide, say, two fingers, by concealing them with your other hand. Ask them to work out how many fingers you are hiding.

● Give the children a number, such as four, and ask them to give you the number before, in this case three.

● Choose six children. Establish with the rest of the group that there are six children all together. Let some of the six children hide without the rest of the group seeing. Show the remainder of the six to the rest of the group, then ask them to say how many are hidden.

● Whenever the circumstances arise, give the children an opportunity to subtract (for example, when one child leaves the group to go to wash their hands, how many remain? When one pencil breaks, how many are still working? When one paint pot is empty, how many still have paint in them? When one child leaves the play house, how many are still in there?)

## Involving parents

Invite parents to ask children questions about subtraction whenever the opportunity arises, for example: 'How many people have finished their dinner?' 'How many still haven't?' 'How many cakes were there?' 'How many are left?' 'If we have five sweets and eat three, how many will be left?' Suggest that they might try this out with real sweets (or slices of fruit, raisins, and so on).

# Finding the difference

## Intended learning

To begin to understand the vocabulary of subtraction; to compare two groups of objects and count on or back from one to the other to find the difference between them.

## Introduction

The word 'difference' has a far more specific meaning in mathematics – particularly in number – than in everyday language. When we ask, 'What is the difference between two and four?' children's everyday language often leads them to respond with answers like: 'Four is made with straight lines, and two has a curve in it,' or, 'You need three lines to make a four.' In the context of number, what we mean is, 'How many more/fewer are there in one group than in the other?' The same result is achieved by taking the smaller number away from the larger. The activities in this section aim to reinforce children's understanding of 'difference' in the mathematical sense.

## Key vocabulary

count back, how many more, how many fewer, difference, compare

## Two sticks

### Group size:
two to six children.

### You will need:
interlocking cubes.

### The activity
Introduce the activity by making two 'sticks', one two cubes longer than the other.

Discuss with the children how many cubes you would have to take off the longer stick to make it the same size as the shorter one. Then ask the children each to make two sticks of cubes, one two cubes shorter than the other. Talk to the children as they work, introducing the term 'difference' where appropriate.

### Extension and differentiation

● Support children by counting with them as they assemble their sticks of cubes.

● If children have difficulty with this activity, let them use sticks of cubes with a difference of just one. Lead them to understand that a stick with one cube more than another has a difference of one, and a stick with one cube less than another also has a difference of one.

● Ask the children to make pairs of sticks with differences of another number.

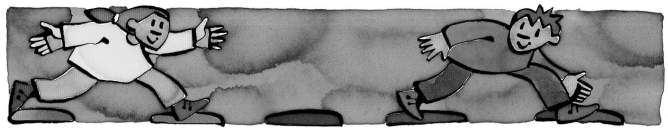

These children quickly learned to work out the difference between the numbers of beads they were holding.

# Make it the same

## Group size:
four to eight children.

## You will need:
conkers (or shells, cubes, counters, and so on).

## The activity
Ask the children to work with a partner. Place a small pile of conkers between each pair, then explain that each child should take a handful of conkers from the pile, show their partner and count how many they each have. If they each have a different number from their partner, ask them to put some back or take some more until they both have the same amount. Repeat the activity a few times.

## Extension and differentiation
● Help the children with counting as necessary. If they are still struggling with the counting, reduce the number of conkers available to them.

● Ask the children to explain to the rest of the group how they made their handfuls the same.

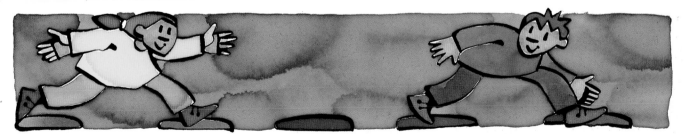

## Catching up

### Group size:
four to eight children.

### You will need:
up to ten large circles of paper; a set of large 0 to 9 number cards.

### The activity
Lay the paper circles across the floor in a wavy line and tell the children that these are stepping stones. Shuffle the number cards and place them in a pile face down on the floor.

Invite two children to stand behind the first stepping stone. Ask them each to pick a number card from the top of the pile and hop along that number of stepping stones. Point out that one child is further along the line than the other, then ask the rest of the group to try to work out how many extra hops the second child needs to take to catch up with the first.

Discuss with the children how they worked it out, then let other pairs of children have a turn at taking cards and hopping.

### Extension and differentiation
● If necessary, use 0 to 5 number cards.

● Ask the child who is ahead how many steps back they would have to take to get to the other child.

● Try the same activity in a different context, such as walking up steps.

## Partners

### Group size:
ten to 12 children.

### You will need:
no special equipment.

### The activity
Count out, say, five children to stand in a row at the front, facing the rest of the group. Ask the remaining children to close their eyes tightly. Very quietly, without the other children realising, invite one or two more children from the group to join the row at the front. Ask the rest of the group to open their eyes and try to work out the difference between the numbers of children.

### Extension and differentiation
● Make the activity simpler by inviting just three children to stand at the front. Then let just one more child join the row.

● Children may find the use of the word 'difference' rather difficult to understand. Emphasise the word, and ask the children to repeat it back to you.

● Give each child in the group a set of number cards to 5. Ask them to find the card that shows the answer, instead of calling it out.

● Choose a larger number of children to stand in the row at the front.

## Assessment

● Can children say how many more/fewer objects they have than another child?

● Can they say how many more/fewer they need in order to have the same number as someone else?

● Do they understand the connection between 'more than' and 'fewer than'?

● Can they use the word 'difference' with accuracy and understanding?

## Evidence of the children's learning

The children's use of the word 'difference' developed most markedly during the game of *Two sticks*. We focused on a 'different difference' each day and the children learnt to complete the sentence 'The sticks have a difference of...' when they saw the two sticks. We further developed the activity by asking the children to make their own pairs of sticks and say their own sentences to describe the difference between them.

As far as possible we interchanged the phrases 'more than', 'fewer than' and 'difference between' in order to establish the connection between the three descriptions.

## Other quick ideas

● Organise the children into two lines side by side. One line should be made up of children who fulfil a particular criterion (for example, wearing cardigans, trainers, white socks or lace-up shoes), while the other line should comprise the rest of the children. Ask what is the difference between the number of children in the lines. Ask the children to hold hands in pairs to check.

● Each day, take every opportunity to ask children questions about finding the difference ('What is the difference between the number of chairs and the number of children?' 'What is the difference between the number of dolls and the number of teddies?' 'What is the difference between the number of fingers I am holding up and the number of fingers you are holding up?').

## Involving parents

Invite parents to ask their children questions about the difference between numbers in a variety of everyday contexts: 'What is the difference between the number of spoons and the number of forks in the drawer?' 'What is the difference between the number of biscuits you want and the number you have?' 'What is the difference between the number of steps Mum takes across the room and the number of steps you take across the room?'

# Money

## Intended learning

To begin to understand and use vocabulary related to money; to begin to recognise coins in role-play situations; to begin to count up to ten.

## Introduction

Money is often a difficult idea for children to understand, even for those who are very numerate. The understanding that one coin can be worth two pence is quite sophisticated and at odds with the one-to-one matching aspect of counting which is emphasised to children at this stage. Until their skills in counting are sound, it is less confusing for the children if they only use pennies for 'shopping' games. These activities help children to develop recognition of coins and their names. Many of them also relate to other units and give the children an opportunity to use the skills they have developed in the context of money.

## Key vocabulary

coin, value, worth, penny, pence, 'p', how much more, how much less

## Special coins

### Group size:
two to six children.

### You will need:
a collection of coins (real coins are best, but if this is absolutely impractical, realistic toy money can be used).

### The activity

Discuss the coins with the children, talking about their similarities and differences in terms of size, colour, shape, edges, pictures, and so on. Pick out a group of coins with a feature in common, such as all the bronze-coloured ones. Explain to the children that this is your special set. Can they guess why? Give them an opportunity to respond, and replace the coins.

Repeat the game, choosing a different group of coins (all the silver-coloured ones or all the ones with corners).

### Extension and differentiation

● Let the children take turns to choose the groups of coins.

● Remind the children of one of the 'sorting diagrams' (see the unit on *Sorting*, pages 32–35). Sort the coins on to an unlabelled diagram, and play the game as before.

## Shopping

### Group size:
four to eight children.

### You will need:
labels; marker pen; ten pennies for each child; a yoghurt pot for each child.

Buying a pencil from the table-top shop

## The activity

Either with the children, or in advance of the activity, set up some table-top 'shops' around the room where the children may 'buy' items they need during the day. For example, you might have shops for pencils, paper, crayons, rulers, scissors and rubbers. Label the items with prices at your discretion, for example, you could charge 1 penny each for everything except paper (2 pence) and rubbers (3 pence). Give each child ten pennies in their own yoghurt pot to spend in the shops whenever you ask them to draw a picture, practise writing, and so on.

## Extension and differentiation

● Restrict the prices to just one penny for all items. Give the children just five pennies to spend.

● Introduce a milk and biscuits 'shop'. The children can place orders for their milk and biscuits during the day. For example, milk could cost 3 pence and biscuits 1 penny each. Make a time for each child to place their order – either by drawing what they want or by telling the teacher. Then ask the children to find the correct number of pennies.

# Jumping pennies

## Group size:
four to eight children.

## You will need:
pennies; a small purse (optional).

## The activity
Hide up to nine pennies in your pocket. Jump on the spot however many times necessary to show the number of pennies you have. The children must guess, or work out from the number of jumps, how many pennies you have. Let them count the pennies to see if they were right.

Once the children understand the game, let them take turns to hide the pennies. You may need to check that the number of pennies and the number of jumps match before the rest of the group are allowed to count the contents of the pocket. If any of the children do not have pockets, provide a small purse instead.

## Extension and differentiation
● For children who are struggling with this activity, use fewer pennies. Jump more slowly and encourage the class to count aloud together as you jump.

● Give each child their own set of number cards and ask them to show the correct card for the number of coins.

● Use other coins (for example, five pence) and jump the appropriate number of times. The children then have to guess the denomination of coin, rather than the number of pennies.

# A handful of coins

## Group size:
two to six children.

## You will need:
a collection of mixed coins; 2cm squared paper.

## The activity
Discuss the different coins with the children, including the numbers on them if appropriate. Ask each child to take a handful of coins and sort them into the different denominations. Then give each child a piece of squared paper and ask them to arrange the coins in rows (to make a graph).

Discuss the outcomes with the children ('Which coins did you have most of?' 'Were there two the same?' 'Which coins did you have fewest of?' 'If you could choose two more coins, what would they be?' 'What would the graph look like then?').

## Extension and differentiation
● It may be preferable to only use two denominations of coins for some children.

● If the children are sufficiently confident with the different denominations of coins, they could be introduced to the different values and invited to try to make a total for each row.

## Assessment
● Can the children point to specific denominations of coins when asked?

● Can the children name the different coins?

## Evidence of the children's learning

The children responded enthusiastically to the *Shopping* game, and often bought far more items than they actually needed, just for the fun of shopping. One shopper was caught explaining to another that 'although we've only got pennies, there's another way you can do this [buy a piece of paper] in the real shops.' When asked, she could explain that she could use a 2p coin – or a 'bigger one' and get some money back!

The children thoroughly enjoyed *Jumping pennies*, which reinforced much of the other work they were doing with numbers by giving it a new context.

## Other quick ideas
● Give the children small envelopes and ask them to put in some 1 pence coins and write the amount of money on the outside.

● Turn the play house into a shop. Use old (clean) food packets and stick price labels on them.

● Give the children access to small collections of mixed coins and let them sort them.

## Involving parents
Ask parents to let their children sort collections of coins. Perhaps occasionally they could let the children hand over the money and collect the change in a shop, or let them have ten pence, then challenge them to find something they can buy with it.

# Glossary

## Addition

A mathematics operation which, at this level, amounts to combining two (or more) groups.

## Attribute

A property, such as colour, shape, or size.

## Cardinal number

A number that indicates the number of objects in a group.

## Carroll diagram

A two- or three-way diagram (invented by Lewis Carroll) used to represent information.

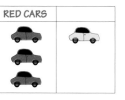

## Conservation of number

The fact that quantities do not change, however they are organised, and that however many times a group of objects is counted, and in whatever order, the outcome will be the same.

## Data

Information, often listed.

## Decimal number

A number based on the use of ten digits.

## Difference

In mathematics specifically, how many more or fewer there are in one group than another.

## Digits

The symbols used to denote numbers 0 to 9.

## Estimate (noun)

An approximate 'informed guess' of a quantity.

## Even number

A whole number which is exactly divisible by two.

## Fewer

'Less' in numerical quantity, for example, I have fewer biscuits than you.

## Less

A smaller amount of something, such as water or sand.

## Number system

Our number system is based on 10. There are others based on different numbers, such as binary, which uses only 0 and 1.

## Numeral

The (collection of) symbols we use to represent numbers.

## Odd number

A whole number that is not divisible exactly by two.

## Ordinal number

A number as it stands in relation to others.

## Pattern

A predictable sequence.

## Place value

The value of a digit according to its place in a number (for example, 2 is worth different amounts in 253 and 52).

## Set

A group.

## Subtraction

A term encompassing 'difference' (the difference when two groups are compared) and 'take away' (the result when one group is removed from another).

## Venn diagram

A way of representing information.

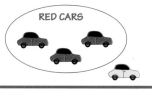

First published 2000 by A & C Black (Publishers) Ltd, 35 Bedford Row, London WC1R 4JH
Text copyright © Janine Blinko 2000. Illustrations copyright © Alison Dexter 2000.
Photographs copyright © Zul Mukhida 2000
The author and publisher wish to thank the staff and children of Knowles Nursery and Knowles First School, Bletchley, Milton Keynes, for their help in the preparation of this book.
ISBN 0-7136-4928-3
A CIP catalogue record for this book is available from the British Library.
Printed in China through Colorcraft Ltd.